Geography Starts

MOUNTAINS

Andy Owen
and
Miranda Ashwell

Heinemann Interactive Library
Des Plaines, Illinois

Published by Heinemann Interactive Library,
an imprint of Reed Educational & Professional Publishing,
Chicago, IL

Customer Service 888-454-2279

Visit our website at www.heinemannlibrary.com

Designed by Susan Clarke

Illustrations by Oxford Illustrators (maps pp.23, 25, 27) and Hardlines (pp.5, 12)
Printed in China

06
10 9 8 7 6

Library of Congress Cataloging-in-Publication Data
Owen, Andy, 1961-
    Mountains / Andy Owen and Miranda Ashwell.
       p.   cm. — (Geography starts)
    Includes bibliographical references and index.
    Summary: An introduction to the types and characteristics of
mountains, including volcanoes and glaciers, and the disastrous
effects on them of landslides and avalanches.
    ISBN 1-57572-607-6 (lib. bdg.)   ISBN 1-58810-976-3 (pbk. bdg.)
    1. Mountains—Juvenile literature.   [1. Mountains.]   I. Ashwell,
Miranda, 1957- .   II. Title.   III. Series: Owen, Andy, 1961-
Geography starts.
GB512.094   1998
551.43'2—dc21   97-34420
                                                             CIP
                                                             AC

Acknowledgments
The Publishers would like to thank the following for permission to reproduce photographs:
Aerofilms, p.15; BBC/David Noton, p.17; Bruce Coleman Ltd, p.4 (Mr Jules Cowan), p.6 (Steven C. Kaufman), p.16
(C.C. Lockwood), p.19 (Dieter & Mary Plage); Environmental Images/Colin Cummings, p.20; Hutchinson, p.8 (Jeremy
Horner), p.9 (Eric Lawrie); Images Colour Library, p.21; Mountain Camera/John Cleare, p.13; Nottingham Trent
University/Tony Waltham, p.18; Robert Harding Picture Library, p.22; Royal Geographical Society, p.28; Sealand Aerial
Photography, pp.24, 26; Still Pictures, p.11 (Georges Lopez), p.14 (Alan Watson); Tony Stone, p.10 (Ernest Braun), p.7
(Paul Chesley), p.29 (Dennis Oda)

Cover photograph: Robert Harding Picture Library

Our thanks to Betty Root for her comments in the preparation of this book.

Some words are shown in bold, **like this**. You can find
out what they mean by looking in the glossary.

Contents

Making Mountains

Mountains are huge chunks of rock that rise above the earth. Some mountains began as **layers** of rock under the sea.

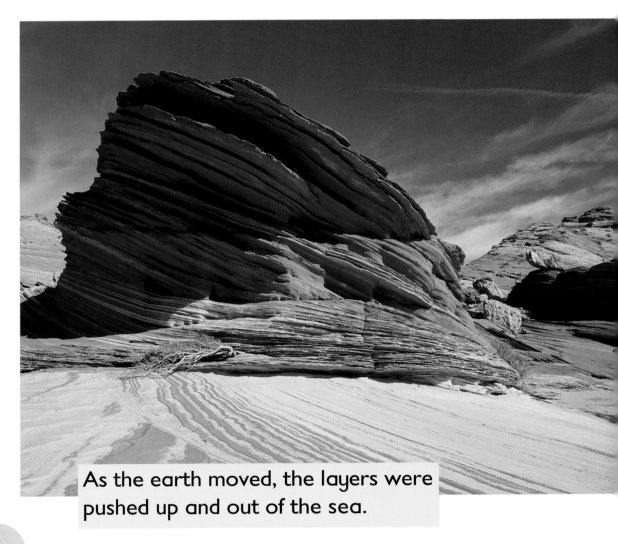

As the earth moved, the layers were pushed up and out of the sea.

Sand and mud fell to the bottom of the sea.

60 million years ago

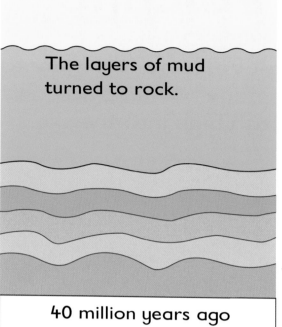

The layers of mud turned to rock.

40 million years ago

The layers were pushed up and the sea got smaller.

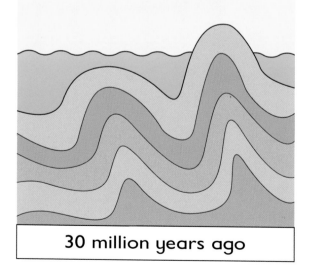

30 million years ago

The rock was pushed into **jagged** shapes above the sea.

20 million years ago

5

Volcano

A **volcano** is a mountain that is still being made. When a volcano **erupts,** it blasts ash high into the sky.

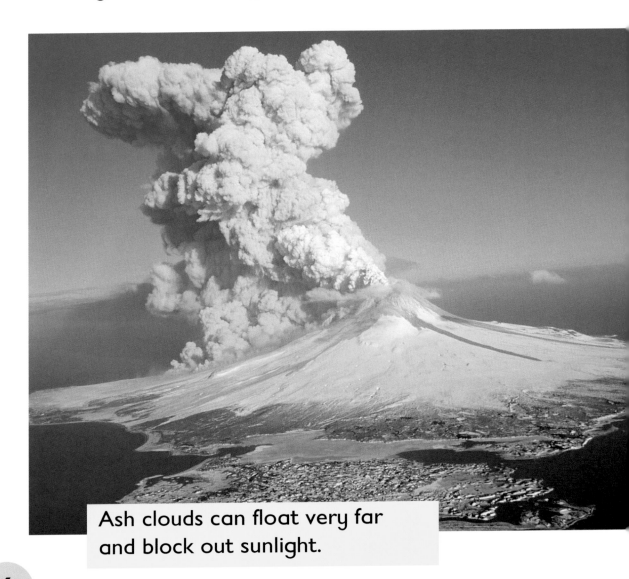

Ash clouds can float very far and block out sunlight.

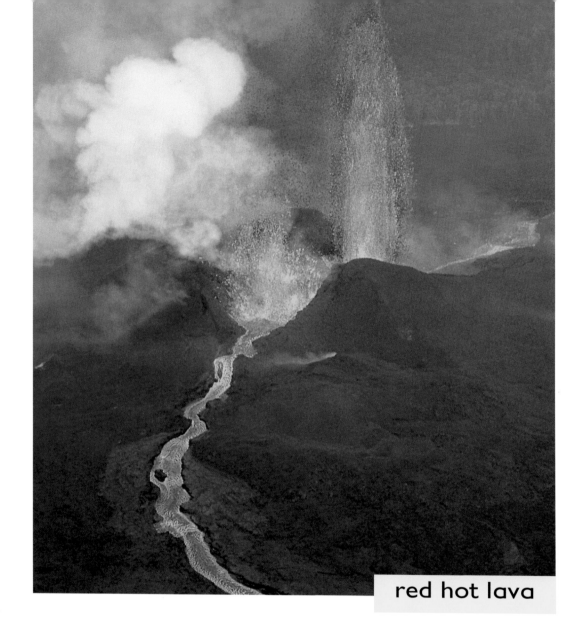

red hot lava

Rocks inside the volcano are so hot that they melt. Melted rock is called lava. Lava is thrown out of the volcano when it erupts.

Sleeping Volcanoes

When a **volcano erupts** it leaves a round hole called a crater. The crater can fill with water and make a lake.

a lake at the top of a volcano

This volcano has not erupted for a long time. Snow covers the cold rocks.

Some volcanoes are quiet for a long time. We say the volcano is dormant, or has been sleeping. Then it may suddenly erupt.

Parts of a Mountain

The foothills are the lowest part of a mountain. Soil covers the rocks so many plants grow here.

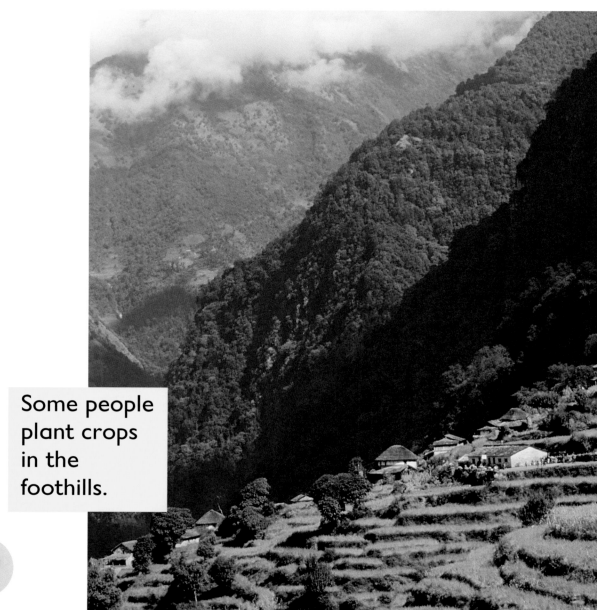

Some people plant crops in the foothills.

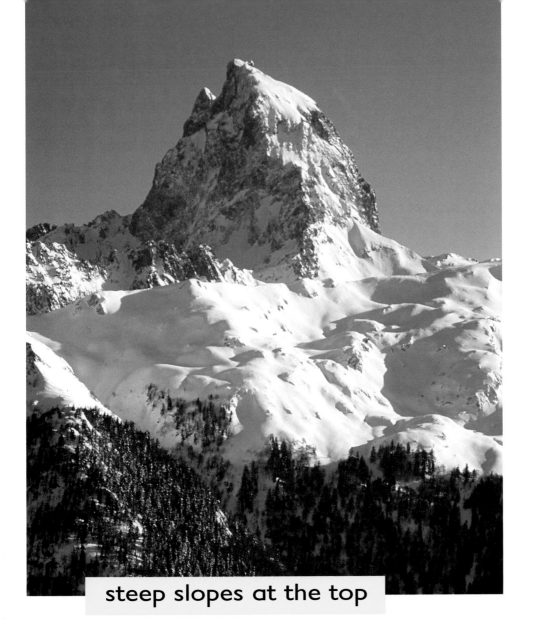

steep slopes at the top

The top of the mountain is called the summit. The summit is often bare rocks with no soil or plants.

Going Up

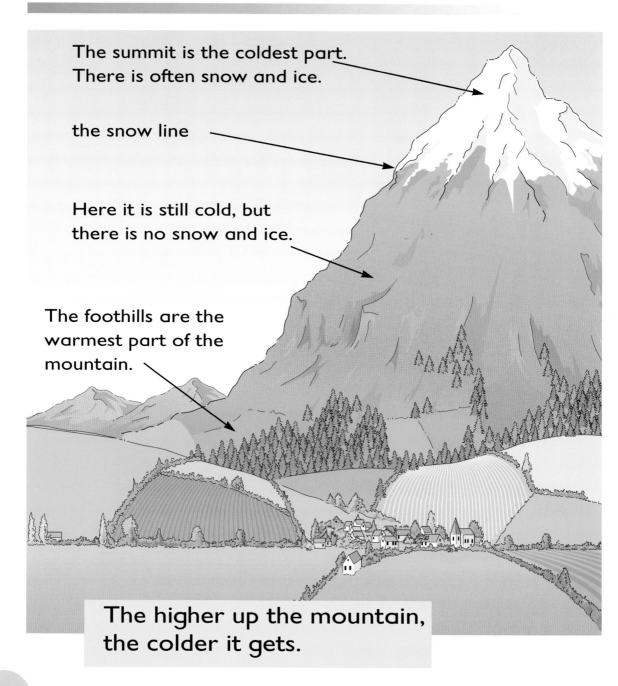

The summit is the coldest part. There is often snow and ice.

the snow line

Here it is still cold, but there is no snow and ice.

The foothills are the warmest part of the mountain.

The higher up the mountain, the colder it gets.

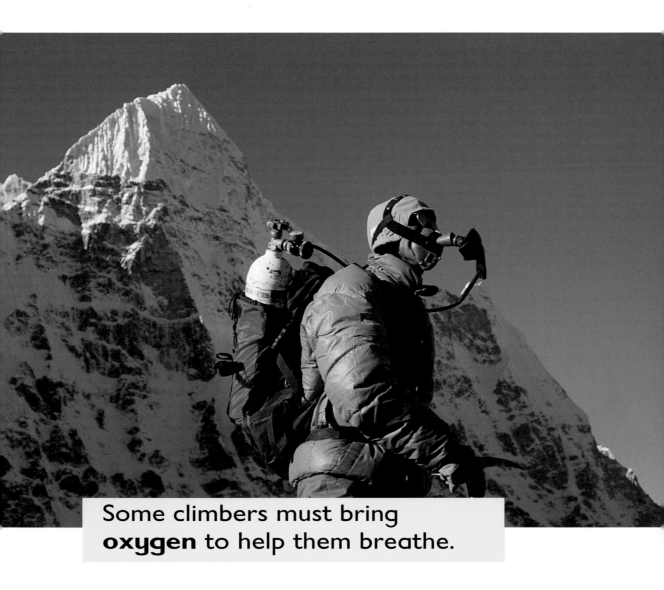

Some climbers must bring **oxygen** to help them breathe.

The air has less oxygen towards the top of a tall mountain. This makes breathing very hard.

Ice on the Mountain

Glaciers are large fields of ice. It takes thousands of years for a glacier to move down a mountain. As it moves, it cuts into the rocks.

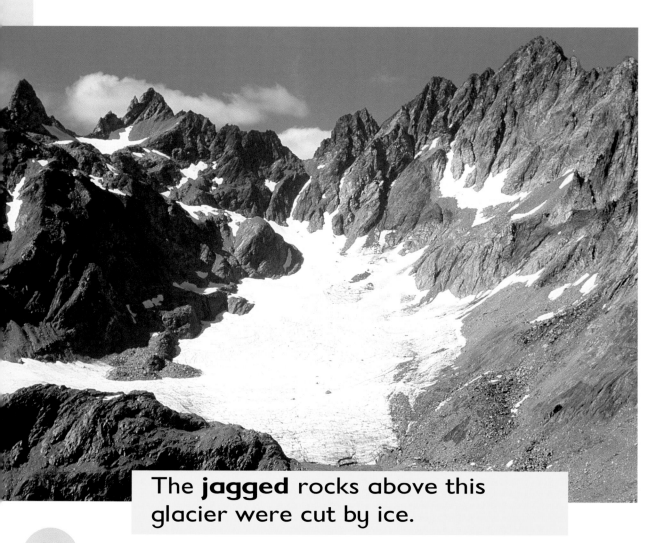

The **jagged** rocks above this glacier were cut by ice.

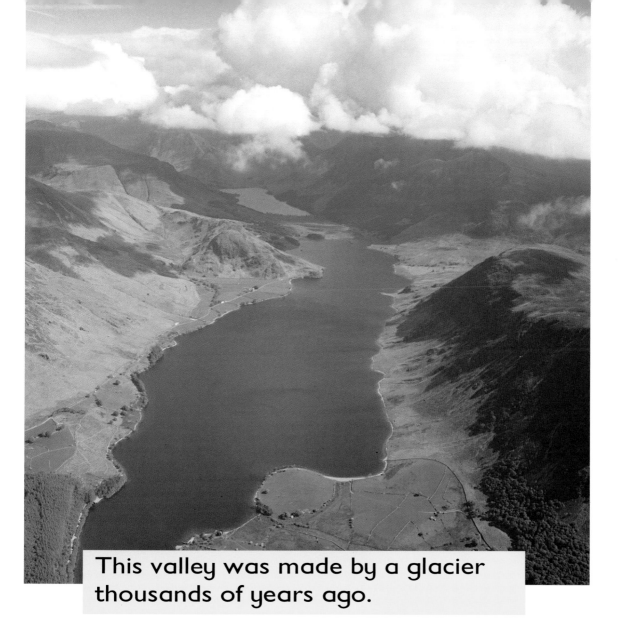

This valley was made by a glacier thousands of years ago.

A **valley** is made when the glacier melts. The steep sides and flat bottom of the valley were made by the moving glacier.

Mountain Water

As water flows down the mountain, it makes a deep cut in the rock called a gorge. It takes thousands of years for a river to make a gorge.

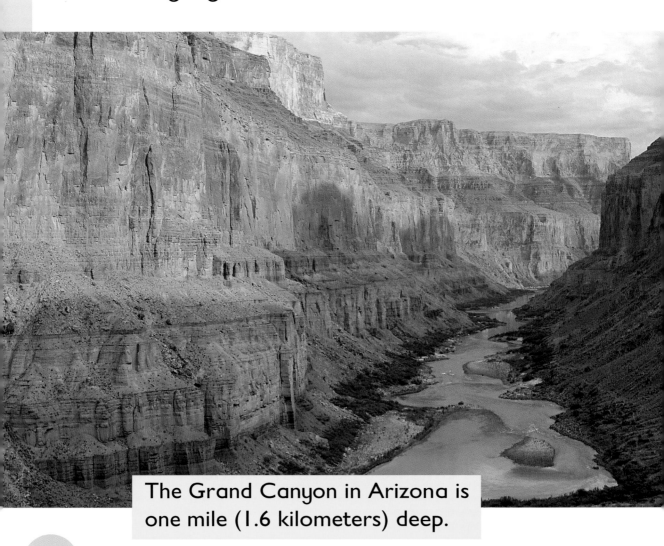

The Grand Canyon in Arizona is one mile (1.6 kilometers) deep.

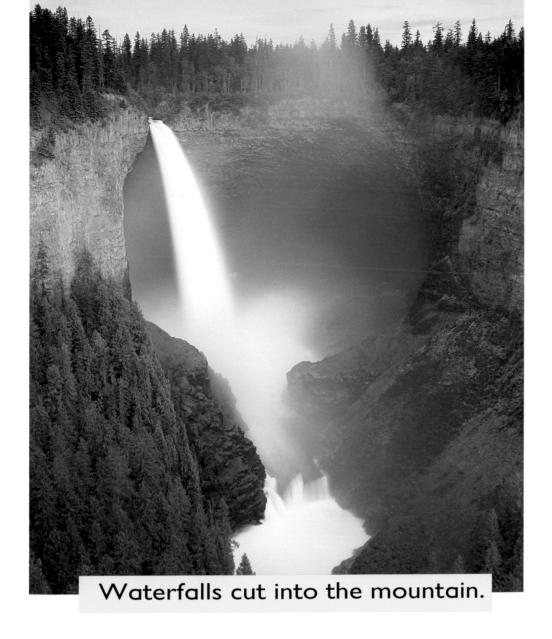

Waterfalls cut into the mountain.

Some steep mountain cliffs are cut by falling water. The mountain is slowly worn down by the moving water.

Desert Mountains

Rocks are warmed by the sun in the day. They cool down at night. This makes the rock crack and break off in **layers**.

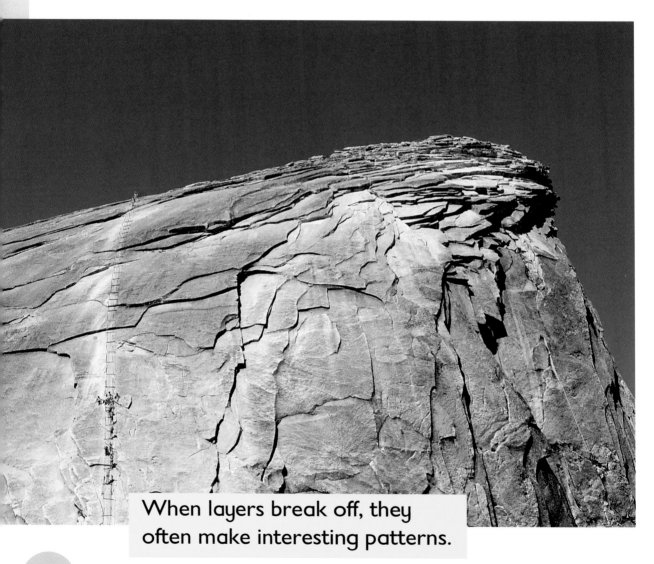

When layers break off, they often make interesting patterns.

These mountains are slowly crumbling.

Some mountains in dry places have flat tops and steep cliffs. In this desert, huge pieces of rock stick out of the desert, like fingers.

Falling Mountains

Large pieces of rock can suddenly break off the mountain side. The rocks tumble and slide down. This is called a landslide.

Landslides can block roads and trap people.

Snow can suddenly fall down steep mountain slopes. This is called an avalanche. An avalanche grows bigger as it tumbles down the mountain.

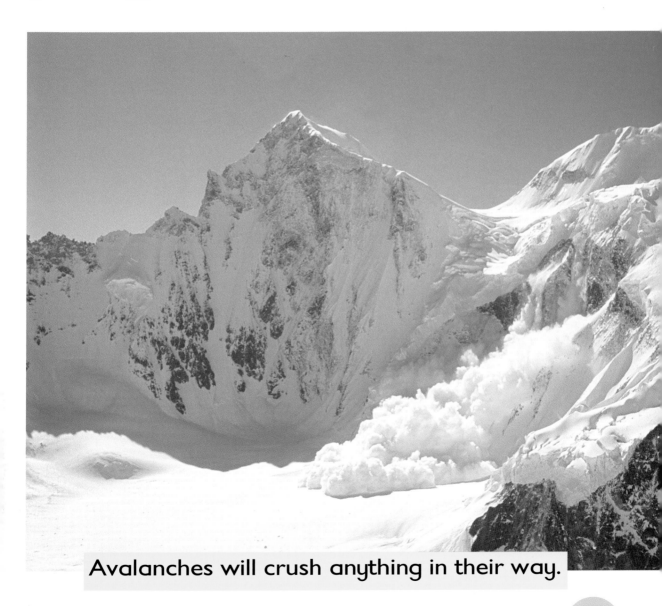

Avalanches will crush anything in their way.

Mountain Map 1

These mountains rise high above the sea. You cannot tell how high a mountain is by looking at a photograph.

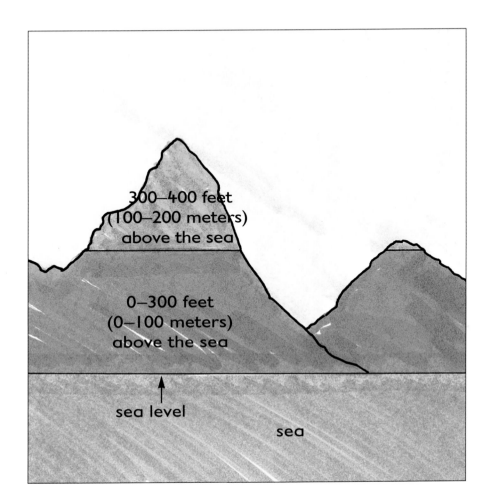

300–400 feet
(100–200 meters)
above the sea

0–300 feet
(0–100 meters)
above the sea

sea level

sea

The colors on this picture show how high the mountains are above the sea.

Mountain Map 2

This photo shows a part of a mountain. It was taken from an airplane. You can see a road leading up to the summit. There is a small lake at the bottom of a steep slope.

The purple color shows the highest part of the mountain. The steep, rocky slopes are shown with short black lines. Brown shows the lowest part where there is a lake.

Mountain Map 3

This photo shows another part of the same mountain. The **valley** is at the bottom of the photo. There is a river and a road in the valley.

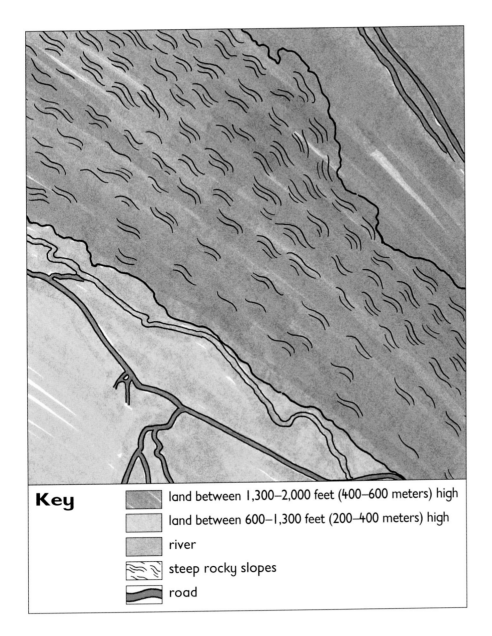

Key		
	▨	land between 1,300–2,000 feet (400–600 meters) high
	▢	land between 600–1,300 feet (200–400 meters) high
	▨	river
	▧	steep rocky slopes
	〰	road

Lines are used to show the road and the river. This map makes it easy to see the fields in the valley.

Amazing Facts

Mount Everest is the highest mountain on land. The first people to climb Everest were Edmund Hillary and Tenzing Norgay in 1953.

The top of Everest is 29,028 feet (8,848 meters) above the sea.

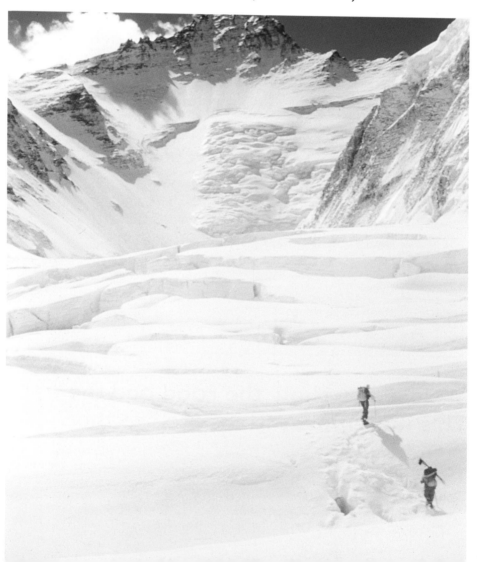

The largest **volcano** in the world is Mauna Loa on the island of Hawaii. It once **erupted** for one and a half years.

Rivers of lava can flow as fast as 550 feet (168 meters) per second.

Glossary

erupts   when hot rocks burst out of a volcano

jagged   having sharp points or edges

layers   thicknesses or levels

oxygen   gas that people, animals, and plants need to live

valley   low land between hills

volcano   opening in the earth where lava comes out, often making a mountain

More Books to Read

Baker, Susan. *First Look at Mountains.* Milwaukee: Gareth Stevens, 1991.

Barrett, Norman S. *Mountains.* New York: Franklin Watts, 1991.

Curran, Eileen. *Mountains and Volcanoes.* Mahwah, NJ: Troll Communications, 1985.

Lye, Keith. *Mountains.* Austin, Tex: Raintree Steck-Vaughn, 1992.

Stone, Lynn. *Mountains.* Danbury, Conn: Children's Press, 1983.

Zoehfeld, Kathleen. *How Mountains are Made.* New York: HarperCollins, 1995.

Index